Elon Musk

A Biography of Billionaire

Entrepreneur Elon Musk

Robert Hanson

Table of Contents

Introduction

"I don't have all the answers. (...) Let me be really clear about that. I'm trying to figure out the set of actions I can take that are more likely to result in a good future. If you have suggestions in that regard, please tell me what they are." - Elon Musk

Nelson Mandela is an iconic figure throughout the world. A gifted Statesman, Nobel Peace Prize recipient, and peacemaker. He is widely regarded as the "Father of the nation" of South Africa. Following his release from prison on Robben Island in 1990, South Africa was on the brink of a civil war that would have resulted in countless deaths and destruction. Mandela however, brokered a peace deal between the white minority who governed South Africa at the time, and the black majority who had for decades been oppressed. This resulted in the first ever democratic election in 1994, when for the first time in South Africa's history, a black man became President.

Despite this positive outcome, there are many today who question the legacy of Nelson Mandela, suggesting that he had in fact failed black people, because the majority of the black population are still living in the same economic circumstances as before 1994. There is even a growing and tangible animosity towards Mandela.

Now one might wonder why Nelson Mandela is featured in the introduction to a book dedicated to Elon Musk. While there is no doubt that Elon would consider it a great honor to be thought of in the same sphere as the Former President, the more pertinent reason is that the history of South Africa preceding and following 1994, is a significant moment in every South African person's life. That fateful day when Nelson Mandela was declared President, forever changed the socio-political narrative of South Africa, and affected every single South African. This was especially the true for those who had lived through this time period. And Elon Musk was one such person. His life would no doubt have turned out very differently, had things progressed other than how they had.

But the legacy of Nelson Mandela also illustrates how relentlessly controversy can pursue someone of an iconic stature. History is teeming with the accounts of men and women who have done many great things but have been dogged by controversy. Greatness attracts controversy, and courts challenge. It is no different for Elon.

There is no denying or escaping the incontrovertible truth that we are confronted with when we take an interest in the life and achievements of Elon Musk. These truths are facts which are unquestionably vital to our gaining an insightful and accurate profile of the man. They can be successfully distilled into three statements concerning our subject:

1. Elon Musk is an extraordinary individual.
2. Elon Musk is a controversial individual.
3. Elon Musk is, nonetheless, still only human.

Elon is Extraordinary

Elon has been involved in the founding of at least four companies that are valued at over a billion dollars each. He is ranked number seven on the Forbes 400, with a net worth of nearly $89 billion as of the 20th of October, 2020. He has been involved in the creation of PayPal, SolarCity, Hyperloop, the Boring Company, and various other business ventures. He is perhaps most famous for single-handedly forcing his way into the automobile industry via Tesla; and into the space-race via SpaceX, and dominating these two fields. He dreams of sustainable and alternative energy sources, and of colonizing space. He has a vision. One which drives him unceasingly towards it's actualization. That vision is to take humanity to the stars.

It is this vision which has allowed him to diversify his business interests across so many different fields and industries, because as he achieves one stage of his vision, he discovers another. If the vision is to colonize Mars, he needs a fleet of spacecrafts to get there. Enter SpaceX. Once SpaceX reaches Mars, there would need to be some form of electric powered transportation due to the almost non-existent levels of oxygen in the atmosphere of Mars. Enter SolarCity and Tesla. In most instances as well, his need to provide affordable products and services has likewise led him to create new businesses in order to self-supply components and products for his existing businesses.

He identifies a need or a deficiency, and then immediately begins working on a solution, either via his own effort and design, or by delegating to the many scientists and capable technicians he employs. The perfect example of this being the Boring Company, the idea for which came to him when he was stuck in a traffic gridlock. The idea was an underground network of tunnels connecting cities, with electric cars traveling at rapid speeds in them.

Wealth, property, multiple businesses, a string of relationships with beautiful actresses and celebrities, are all the order of the day. It is therefore no surprise that in order to help him portray a successful, intelligent and powerful CEO, Robert Downey Jr. based his character of Tony Stark in the "Iron Man" movies on Elon, with one of his factories even being used as the headquarters for the villain in the second movie. Such is the extraordinary life that Elon Musk has built for himself.

Elon is Controversial

Elon became a father for the seventh time recently, with his partner C—the artist formerly known as Grimes, born Claire Boucher—when she gave birth to their son, whom they named "X Æ A-12." As a name with a number could not be registered in California, they changed it to "X Æ A-Xii". This story clearly accounts for some of the controversy that has trailed behind Elon over the years. Coming across at times as abrasive, aloof, and also robotic has merely added more substance to the global perception of Elon as being difficult.

His former wife, Justine, once stated, "Extreme success results from an extreme personality and comes at the cost of many other things." Surprisingly, Elon actually agreed with his then-wife, as he reasoned that it's impossible to colonize Mars working only 40 hours a week. Eventually this social obtuseness would give rise to his issues with the United States Securities and Exchanges Commission (SEC), as well as the later lawsuit filed for defamation, following the cave rescue incident of July 2018.

Elon does not dumb himself down or choose his words carefully. This gets him into trouble, but it falls back on one of his core beliefs as an entrepreneur. Elon firmly believes in being transparent and upfront in everything he does. He actualizes this belief by offering open-source schematics to his ideas, so others can contribute to making them better, and by criticizing companies he works with for withholding information about their operations. This code helps him when it comes to business but hurts him when it comes to social etiquette. Elon is not a fan of self-censorship, and this can get him into trouble. Like many, he is quick to go to Twitter and get his thoughts out into the public from his mouth, before they can be twisted by the public. This is an impulsive habit, and it tends to shine light on his more problematic decisions.

The fact of the matter is that Elon is as fascinating as he is because of these controversial incidents, alongside his natural genius. Through his multiple eccentricities, Elon garners attention to his technological enterprises, and to the causes he cares most about. Every time he makes the news for saying something outrageous or doing something the public does not quite understand, he gets people talking about the future, and that makes people more likely to act on the same problems he wishes to solve.

Elon is Human

Despite the robotic way in which he operates at times, the emotionless front he maintains, the abrasive and aggressive way he often responds to challenges in life, despite all these personality traits and confrontations that he has had both privately and publicly, Elon is still only human. He has experienced the same pain, trauma, joy, happiness, success, sadness, and terror that every other human being has experienced. He is no different. He is very much the result of genetic and hereditary factors, as well as the environmental and circumstantial factors experienced during his childhood and adolescence. And of course, as with any one of us, his adult social interactions. Like all of us, he is a product of living. He does the best that he can in any situation, within the parameters of his personality, and against the demands of his vision.

For all of the incredible things Elon Musk does in the public eye, under approval or scrutiny, he has seven children. He works 80-100 hours a week at times, managing several companies, tech projects, and running a family. People from all parts of the industry come to him for ideas, advice, and financial aid, and this can impact his personal life along the way. Elon is often cited as being a workaholic and spends less time with his family than he'd like. The fact that he has achieved, and continues to achieve so much, is motivating and awe-inspiring for many.

Chapter 1: Meeting Elon Musk

It is certainly true to say that Elon Musk is a controversial and yet fascinating individual. When one considers his many achievements and great legacy, it is all too easy to attribute an almost deity-like quality to him, and thus, to be taken by surprise by his all-too-familiar and very human upbringing. Elon is very much the product of his childhood as any other person would be; however, he might be uniquely so. After all, there are perhaps only a handful of individuals in the world who have even come close to rivaling his enormous successes. So, in some respects he is like any other individual; but in other respects, he is very much unique.

That uniqueness has seen him become the architect of an empire that has dominated every field in which it has taken root. He has created a mammoth multi-corporation, which shows no signs of ever slowing. But what is it that has driven him to pursue all of these interests and enterprises? What is it that drives Elon Musk? What has cemented his passion for enhancing the quality of human life? What has inspired him to pursue living among the stars, on far-away planets? To search for clean and sustainable energy sources? And at the same time, what has so terrified and disturbed him about humanity, that he fears both its destructive ways, but also its pending destruction?

In this we can readily distinguish two vital facts that drive Elon. Firstly, that he has a clear vision, and that vision involves the exploration and colonization of space, and the development of alternative energy sources. But a vision is merely a response. It is a resulting plan to counter some cause or trigger. Having a vision to become fit and healthy, is a response to feeling unfit and unhealthy. Having a vision or goal to promote recycling, means that the current level of recycling is insufficient. And so secondly, Elon's vision is a response to his fears of humanity's destruction.

There are numerous psychological theories and models that exist to explain the development of the personality, of worldviews, morals, drives, and behavior. Where they all agree, is that it is the interaction between genetics and the environmental factors which affects one's upbringing that sets these foundations in place. So, what hereditary and childhood influences have laid the foundations for Elon, and molded him into the man that we now know? What has laid upon him the tasks and burdens that he bears? Most importantly, what has created the vision that he feels so compelled to strive towards?

A Child is Born

Elon was born on the 28th of June, 1971, to Errol and Maye Musk, and was the eldest of their three children. His siblings, Tosca and Kimbal, have likewise also achieved their own individual levels of success and recognition. Errol was an extraordinarily gifted engineer from South Africa, and Maye was a dietician and model from Canada, who lived in South Africa as well. The family lived in Pretoria, and for the first eight years of his childhood, Elon rarely saw either parent. As kids, Elon and his siblings were raised by their housekeeper. While the siblings have always enjoyed and maintained a close and affectionate relationship amongst each other, their experiences with their housekeeper seemed to be a rather cold and sterile one.

Elon's Childhood

It's fair to say that Elon Musk's youth is fascinating to his fans and critics alike. As a famous billionaire, modern images of Elon don't exactly reflect his roots. After growing up in the heart of poverty, racial warfare, and political strife, his eccentric personality shows he had a unique upbringing. Genius minds do not always need to come out of trauma in order to strive, but in Elon's childhood, this was unfortunately the case.

Many aspects of Elon's history highlight his struggle, but when asked about it, he often focuses on what he got out of it all. When his surroundings involved violence, social unrest, and familial abuse, he managed to focus on growing his mind. Using books and education to occupy himself during emotional toil lead him to an undying focus on learning throughout life. As an adult, Elon has carried this with him, giving him a talent for turning tragedy into success.

Living in South Africa

Elon was born during the height of South Africa's Apartheid regime. Apartheid, which means 'apartness' in the Afrikaans language, was a systemic attempt by the National Party of South Africa—in power since 1948—to segregate the white and nonwhite populations of the country.

There is no doubt that being exposed to the worst of human behavior during Apartheid would have indelibly left its mark on his soul. This exposure could possibly be one of the foundational pillars in forming his earnest desire to save humanity. Many years later, around the age of 17, he obtained his passport and fled South Africa for Canada, as he did not wish to support the Apartheid regime through conscription, which was compulsory military service.

Living with His Father

Growing up with his siblings, the family lived in Pretoria, the capital city of South Africa. During an interview with Rolling Stone, he describes his father, Errol Musk, as having a significantly high IQ and as a brilliant and gifted engineer, who supposedly was the youngest South African at the time to qualify as a professional engineer. Errol Musk, in separate interviews with Forbes and the Daily Mail, describes himself as a pilot, sailor, and property consultant who made money developing properties. Before the age of 30, he was already a millionaire who drove his kids to school in a convertible Rolls-Royce. The children grew up riding horses, and had their own motorbikes by age 14. In fact, according to Errol, the family was full of adventures and achievers. His grandmother was the first chiropractor in Canada, and his parents were the first to fly from South Africa to Australia in a single-engine plane.

Errol admits that while he loved the children's mother, through his own infidelities, they separated after 16 years of marriage when Elon was around the age of eight. From this point on, father and son's accounts of the next nine years differ considerably. The siblings were to remain in their mother's custody following the separation, but Elon felt sympathy for his father, whom he thought of as lonely and alone; and so opted to rather remain with his father in Lone Hill, which was a suburb in Johannesburg where his father stayed. This was a decision that he would soon come to regret.

Living with Fear and Brilliance

Elon came to realize that living with his father would not be easy, let alone pleasant. He came to see his father as an incredibly evil and violent man, who constantly came up with new ways to perpetuate evil. His father was a wholly terrible person in his eyes, often subjecting him to hours of lectures. According to Elon, his childhood was one of pain and isolation, with a cold and distant father, who when present, would belittle his interest in computers and science. Elon has never truly elaborated on the nature of the evil his father was capable of; but whatever form it ultimately took, recalling it brought him to tears during an interview with Rolling Stone.

From his father's perspective, Errol has denied ever physically abusing any of the kids. He has consented to enforcing corporal punishment on them when they were young; however, this was not in an excessive or abusive way. He explains that the hours of lectures he forced his son to endure, were to pass on wisdom. Life in Apartheid South Africa was a battleground to ensure a business was successful and survived. He furthermore implied that any perceived harshness in his parenting style and abrasiveness in his personality would also be due to his military conscription as a young man. South African conscription was indeed a turbulent experience on any young South African psyche. He denies discouraging Elon from pursuing his interests in science and computers, and in fact maintains that he encouraged Elon in this regard.

Errol insists that he is misunderstood and often vilified by many. He is not violent, nor aggressive, though admits he was once charged with manslaughter for killing three intruders. Subsequently though, he was acquitted of all charges on the grounds that he had acted in self-defense. Consequently, he considers this legal matter to be the likely cause of Elon's accusations of violence and evil. He has even gone so far as to suggest that Elon should grow up and stop acting like a spoilt child, implying that his accusations are false.

Regardless of whether or not Errol agrees with his son's version of events, the truth is that Elon believes them to be accurate. Therefore, his traumatic childhood with his father has been viewed by many as a significant foundational pillar in creating the entrepreneur and visionary that we know him as today.

Living with Science and Books

The one thing that both father and son agree on, is that Elon was completely smitten with science, computers, and books. His favorite books were science fiction novels by Isaac Asimov, particularly the Foundation Series, which is about a massive galactic empire that is about to be decimated, and the actions and plans to save the empire. This storyline is widely held to be the prime foundation of Elon's belief in the future termination of humanity, and his intense desire and urgency to save humanity and in the process, better the lives of his fellow man. It is what seems to drive all of his projects and passions.

Growing up with a housekeeper who merely monitored the kids, and parents who were both focused on their respective careers, meant that Elon was often left to his own devices and self-interests. It was this freedom that led him firstly to books and the Asimov series, but secondly, also afforded him the opportunities to experiment with science. While other kids played with marbles, sticks, and chalk on sidewalks, Elon was making rockets and explosives. Having a father who was a gifted and highly talented engineer meant that engineering came very easily to the younger Musk, who had a clear proclivity towards science and computers.

When he was 11-years old, Elon pleaded with his father to enroll him in a computer course at the University of the Witwatersrand in Johannesburg. It was a three-hour long course, featuring prominent computer experts from the UK, discussing the future of computers. Much to his joy, his father enrolled him. After the course had ended, Errol and younger brother Kimbal entered the room where the lecture had been held—looking for Elon—and found him in the center of a discussion with all the experts. One of the professors simply told Errol to secure a computer for Elon.

Thankfully, this was exactly what he did, and on that very computer Elon taught himself how to code at age 11. About a year later, he sold the very first game he had created called Blastar to a computer magazine.

Living with School and Bullying

When Elon was around 15-years of age, Errol entered his bedroom one evening and found a strange device on his son's desk. Without any fuss, Elon explained that it was a modem that one day will be in every house, and that it will allow the entire world to be connected. While Elon's scientific mind was blossoming, his social life was certainly not.

Elon was the smallest and youngest in his class at Pretoria Boys High School and was known for being part of the computer club and rather bookish. Throughout his time there, Elon was subjected to severe bullying. He has described this period as extremely difficult but offers advice to young people facing similar problems today.

When describing a particular fight, he recounts confronting a bully that was prepared to beat him senseless. He reportedly went up to the kid, punched him hard enough in the nose that it knocked him out, and got him off his back for good.

Elon was quoted as saying "It taught me a lesson: If you're fighting a bully, you cannot appease a bully. (...) You punch the bully in the nose. Bullies are looking for targets that won't fight back. If you make yourself a hard target and punch the bully in the nose, he's going to beat the shit out of you, but he's actually not going to hit you again."

On one occasion he even needed to be hospitalized following a brutal encounter, where he was thrown down a flight of stairs, and beaten until he blacked out. This final assault prompted him to conclude that enough was enough. Following a growth spurt, as well as taking up judo, karate, and wrestling, he started defending himself and fighting back against his bullies, who consequently ceased targeting him.

Leaving South Africa

After living with his father for almost nine years, Elon decided that his future would best be established by pursuing his academic studies abroad. His desire was to study in America, and likewise to gain citizenship there. This, he thought, would be easier to acquire with his mother's ancestral visa to Canada. And so, at the age of 17, after graduating from school, he moved to Ontario in Canada, and enrolled at Queen's University in Kingston.

At the same time, this also allowed him the opportunity to avoid the conscription mandate in South Africa. Conscription was a military service that was instituted in 1957 and made compulsory from 1968 onwards. It mandated all school-leaving white males to complete their military service training. Failure to do so was a criminally punishable offense. The National Government at that the time believed that in order to secure its rule, it needed to ensure that the white population supported its attempts to control and subjugate the nonwhite population, and so the military service was seen as the ideal tool to foster the 'us' versus 'them' mentality.

Not wishing to support the Apartheid regime, his opportunity to study abroad provided the perfect excuse to avoid the call-up. Once settled in Canada, he immediately applied for passports for his mother, brother, and sister to also leave South Africa and settle in Canada, albeit temporarily. According to Elon, his father offered no support, or even congratulations, or well-wishes. Instead he insisted that Elon was an idiot, who was doomed to fail, and would return within three months, because he was incompetent. This would no doubt have served as a powerful motivator for him, the desire to prove his father wrong, and to achieve all that he envisioned.

Chapter 2: Building Blocks - Starting an Empire

"I try to do useful things... That's a nice aspiration. And useful means it is of value to the rest of society. Are they useful things that work and make people's lives better, make the future seem better, and actually are better, too? I think we should try to make the future better" - Elon Musk

This has truly been the mantra of Elon's life. Identifying a means to enhance or better the human experience, and at a reasonable cost so that the average individual can afford it. Perhaps of the utmost importance to him as well, is his desire to source alternative energy sources that are sustainable, and not harmful to the environment, as fossil fuels are. He has even gone so far as to allow his numerous patents to remain in the public domain, as this is, in his opinion, the only way to ensure the proliferation of such designs, and that his fellow corporates would likewise invest in them.

Beginning his journey towards success and achieving these goals, brought Elon to Canada and Queen's University in Kingston, Ontario. With his mother and siblings with him, and no consideration from his father other than disdain, he remained at the university for two years before transferring to the University of Pennsylvania, in Philadelphia.

At this time, his father even attempted to convince him to attend school in South Africa, to stay within the country. Elon refused this, not simply to reject his father's control, but because he knew he would be more successful in North America. He had dreams to start business and advance technology with research that was starting to get exciting in American schools. He would go on to graduate from the university with bachelor's degrees in Physics and Economics.

Becoming a Millionaire for the First Time

During his time at the university of Pennsylvania, Musk demonstrated his resourcefulness and business acumen, when he and classmate, Adeo Ressi, rented a 10-bedroom fraternity house and converted it into a nightclub, which had around 1,000 patrons a night. According to Ressi, now also a successful entrepreneur and investor, Elon was not at all interested in the social aspects of the nightclub, but saw it basically as an experiment, and a means to cover their tuition fees. Most of his time was spent in his room, playing video games while the partying happened downstairs.

After graduating, Elon then enrolled in a Ph.D. program in Applied Physics at Stanford University in California; however, he dropped out of the course after only two days. His interests and keen mind had been drawn in by the internet boom. Along with his brother Kimbal, they co-founded Zip2.

Starting Zip2

Elon explains that his desire was never to make money or to pursue wealth. His intention behind Zip2 was simply to harness the internet. At that time there was, in any event, no wealth to pursue in building the internet. In his mind, the internet was a more useful tool for changing society than working in physics. That was his motivation. Zip2 was designed to be an online directory and city-mapping platform for online newspapers and magazines. He had the backing of numerous Silicon Valley investors to fund the endeavor.

The platform was Java-based, and because they had only one computer, they ran the website during the day, while at night Elon wrote the code. While the business was still growing, Elon lived in the office they rented at Palo Alto, and used the bathroom facilities of the nearby YMCA. At this time, he also experienced his first brush with challenges in the business world. Wanting to be appointed as the CEO, the board of directors prevented this from happening. The hard work and challenges of a start-up paid off eventually, as computer manufacturer Compaq bought Zip2 for US$307 million in cash. This made

Elon a millionaire for the first time, as he earned US$22 million for his 7% shareholding.

An Upward Trajectory

Following his success and the millions he received from the sale of Zip2, Elon's next big move was to invest in a new venture that would truly herald his foray into the big leagues of industry. Without a doubt, his next move would take him to the dizzying heights he has been most associated with over the years, and mold him into the man who would come to stand at the center of both the extraordinary but also the controversial.

X.com

Using $10 million of the payment he received from the sale of Zip2, he co-founded an online banking and email payment company called X.com in 1999. X.com offered something that had never been seen before, namely the opportunity to email money to a friend. Just how successful and popular this novel concept proved to be, was seen just one year later.

PayPal

In the year 2000, X.com merged with another recently created company called Confinity, which had been co-founded by Peter Thiel, Luke Nosek, and Max Levchin. Confinity had minor success with an electronic payment platform they had created called PayPal. Following the merger, Elon was very enthusiastic about the PayPal system, and felt that it had the potential to be lucrative, and that the newly merged company should prioritize further developing it. The CEO at the time however, disagreed, and so left the company.

At this point, Elon was appointed as the new CEO, which turned out to be a rather short-lived appointment. In October 2000, Elon was pushing for a change in PayPal's operating system. He wanted to move their servers away from the free Unix-based operating system to a Microsoft-based one. The board, and especially Max Levchin, did not support his plan. And so, while Elon was vacationing in Australia, the board met and fired him as CEO, replacing him with Peter Thiel as the new CEO. Elon did retain his membership on the board, however. Shortly thereafter the company was renamed as PayPal in 2001, and went public in 2002.

eBay

Ultimately, Elon did come out victorious, at least financially. In October 2002, PayPal was acquired by eBay for US$1.5 billion. Elon, the largest shareholder with 11.7% shares, received US$165 million. This would not be the last encounter he would have with X.com. In 2017, he bought the domain name X.com for an undisclosed amount of money, stating that it had sentimental value for him.

Stars and Planets

If Elon learnt one lesson from his experiences with Zip2 and PayPal, it's that unless you are fully in control of a company, either your vision can be ousted, or you yourself can be ousted. That would not happen again. His vision was the fuel behind all his endeavors. His belief that the future of humanity was threatened, and that any one of a number of different potential threats could end humanity, is what inspired him to pursue his vision. Growing up with a love and adoration for science fiction, comics, and fantasy, he appreciated the importance of space exploration. In order for humanity to survive, he believes that we have to become space explorers and dwellers. Mars is the most likely candidate planet for colonization. This conviction has led him to invest his time, mind, and considerable wealth into space travel, which gave rise to a very interesting space-based experiment he envisioned, called Mars Oasis.

Mars Oasis

Arguably that which Elon is most well-known and popular for, is privatizing space travel. Even before the PayPal sale had happened, he was already contemplating the future of space travel. Elon was disillusioned by both the pace and cost involved in sending rockets into space. He also wanted to reignite the waning interest in space travel, for the simple reason that he felt that was where humanity's future lay. And so, he devised a plan to send a greenhouse to Mars, in the hopes of involving NASA, but also to revitalize interest in space travel, and thus secure additional funding for NASA. The project was titled Mars Oasis, and the aim was to land a greenhouse on the surface of Mars that would be capable of thriving on the planet.

"I went to NASA's website to see when we were going to Mars, but I couldn't find that out... The first idea I had was to send a small greenhouse to Mars... That would get people excited. The whole purpose of that was to get people excited about sending people to Mars and increase NASA's budget."

Realizing that NASA had no plans or resources for the project he envisioned, he travelled to Russia to purchase refurbished ICBM rockets. Travelling along with his best friend from College, Adeo Ressi, and also Jim Cantrell, an aerospace supplies fixer, the mission was a complete failure. Following a second trip a few months later, Elon again met with disappointment. On the trip back to the US, he then realized and calculated that the actual costs of manufacturing the rockets were miniscule in comparison to the selling price. And so, he devised a new project. A new business venture: they would build their own rockets, in order to transport their planned payloads into space. In order to realize Mars Oasis, he needed to build his own rockets. And so, he poured US$100 million of his own wealth into founding Space Exploration Technologies Corp. otherwise known as SpaceX.

SpaceX

In May 2002, Elon founded SpaceX in Hawthorne, California, with the specific intention of manufacturing rockets at a considerably cheaper rate. His intention was to reduce the cost of space travel by a factor of at least 10, so as to be able to successfully colonize Mars. Over the next few years, SpaceX developed their own space transport systems. They named their rockets after the Millennium Falcon from the Star Wars franchise, the Falcon 1 and the Falcon 9. Their capsule or spacecraft was named the Dragon, as a jab at their sceptics who taunted that SpaceX would never be able to put vehicles in space. In 2006, SpaceX was awarded a contract along with another agency to resupply the International Space Station (ISS), followed by a contract for US$1.5 billion in 2008 from NASA, to handle cargo transport to the ISS, with planned crew transport in the future. This would mean replacing NASA's decommissioned shuttle. That same year, the Falcon 1 became the first privately owned rocket to achieve orbit; while in 2010, the Dragon became the first privately owned capsule to be launched, achieve orbit, and to be recovered.

Four years after being awarded the NASA contract, the Dragon was sent to the ISS with 1,000 pounds of supplies. This would be the first time ever that a private company would send a spacecraft to dock at the ISS. Following this momentous event, SpaceX would proceed to set many more new records and firsts.

In December 2013, a Falcon 9 was able to place a satellite into geosynchronous transfer orbit around the earth, thus travelling on earth's rotation. This would have a significant impact on one of the next companies Elon would start.

In 2014, SpaceX was awarded a contract to transport astronauts to the ISS, and to develop the Dragon 2 Crew capsule. The following year, the Deep Space Climate Observatory (DSCOVR) was launched on yet another Falcon 9, in order to monitor the extreme radiation from the sun, which affects the power grids and communication systems on earth.

Elon then believed that the next big challenge and cost-reducer would be making the rockets reusable, a feat which industry experts had deemed impossible. In December 2015, as was to be expected, Elon proved the industry experts wrong. A Falcon 9 rocket achieved the first ever vertical take-off and vertical propulsive landing (VTVL), landing securely and upright on its launchpad. They would also be the first company to VTVL land a rocket in the middle of the ocean, on an automated spaceport drone-boat. This VTVL landing would go on to be repeated numerous times, with almost half of all rockets launched being recovered.

In 2018, SpaceX unveiled their newest rocket, the Falcon Heavy, which was armed with additional Falcon 9 boosters, and could transport a massive 117,000 pounds of cargo into space, which was almost twice as much as its competitor, the Boeing Delta IV Heavy. It also could achieve this at almost a third of the cost. The Falcon Heavy was also designed with potential deep space missions in mind. The inaugural mission's dummy payload was Elon's own cherry-red Tesla Roadster, which was fitted with a camera in the hopes of "some epic views" of the trip around the sun.

Mars and Starship

Because of his belief in the pending destruction of humanity, Elon has focused all of his resources towards colonizing Mars. His goal is to have humans on Mars sometime in the 2020s, with a colony established by 2040, housing up to 80,000 settlers. Given Mars' lack of oxygen, he believes all transportation will need to be electric-based, which would explain the next major industry he has captured, electric motor vehicles. In 2016, Elon outlined his plans to achieve just this goal. Elon aimed for the first unmanned trip to Mars to be in 2022, while the first manned trip would be in 2024.

The successor to the Falcon rockets will be the Big Falcon Rocket (BFR), which would be capable of supporting all SpaceX transport vehicles. This would replace the Falcon 9, the Falcon Heavy, and the Dragon vehicles as a two-stage system, incorporating a booster and a capsule. In 2018, BFR was renamed the Super Heavy-Starship system. The first stage, or booster, was named Super Heavy, while the capsule or spacecraft, was named Starship. As a two-stage Interplanetary Transport System, it was intended for interplanetary transporting of crews. Super Heavy can carry a whopping 220,000 pounds into earth orbit, while the second-stage Starship can provide fast transportation between Earth, Mars, and the Moon.

The thought behind Starship is to ensure that the entire system is reusable and recoverable to minimize space travel costs. The sheer magnitude of Elon's vision and goals is only further magnified when considering that his role in SpaceX was not only as the CEO. In addition to being CEO of SpaceX, Musk was also chief designer in building the Falcon rockets, Dragon, and Grasshopper. Grasshopper was a Falcon 9 prototype.

Chapter 3: Expansion, Challenges, and More

Having already experienced the challenges that came with founding Zip2 and PayPal, Elon's experience with opposition and obstacles would only snowball as his popularity and global identity grew. And his global presence and dominance definitely was growing. "All things serve the beam" is a well-known phrase in Stephen King's seminal works, The Dark Tower series. The beam represents a very powerful and physical manifestation of existence itself, which is in turn represented by a great Tower. The phrase therefore illustrates the idea that everything in the King universe exists to serve that beam. And in the same way, in Elon's universe, all things serve the vision. Every company, every design, and every idea he has ever formulated, has its purpose in serving his vision of saving humanity. Everything he has ever done, moves him one step closer each time towards realizing his vision.

Zip2 allowed him to acquire PayPal, the sale of which provided a massive fortune which enabled him to create SpaceX. SpaceX gave him the physical means of travelling through space. Now, he needed capable and electrically operated vehicles that could function on Mars. He needed satellite communication that was stable and reliable. He needed a habitat that would likewise be able to thrive with alternative and sustainable energy.

The formation and successes of SpaceX were nothing more than a catalyst for the next two major companies that he would be forming, namely Starlink and Tesla. As he worked tirelessly on his vision, the first cracks and creases of opposition were starting to form.

Starlink

Building on the extraordinary achievements of SpaceX, the next step was communication. Elon wished to ensure the widespread proliferation of internet access across the world. Starlink was the next project that he focused his mind towards.

Established in 2015, Starlink was a constellation of low Earth orbit satellites built with the express purpose of providing basic broadband internet access to the entire world, but especially to low income and rural areas. It was also to compete with and break up any monopolies overcharging in certain areas. In March 2018, SpaceX received permission for the US Government to launch two prototype Starlink test-flight satellites into Earth low orbit.

The following year in May 2019, SpaceX sent out the first batch of 60 satellites from its satellite manufacturing plant in Redmond, Washington. This initial deployment was followed by another 60 in November. Elon saw this as a massive success for the Starlink venture; however, many astronomers were unhappy that space was being cluttered with bright and noisy objects that could potentially hinder their observations and study of distant objects in space.

In response to these concerns, SpaceX lowered the orbital height of the satellites, to allow for more unobscured space observation, and also ensured that all subsequent satellites launched will have anti-reflective coating, and also experimental sunshade screens.

The total cost of the project was estimated to be in the region of about US$10 billion. SpaceX will sell some of the satellites for military, scientific, and exploratory research. Currently, SpaceX has permission to launch a total of 42,000 satellites into Earth orbit.

Tesla

Elon's attention next turned to Tesla Motors, a motor vehicle manufacturer and clean energy company based in Palo Alto, California. In time, the company name would change to Tesla inc. The company was incorporated in July of 2003 by Martin Eberhard and Marc Tarpenning, who named the company 'Tesla' as a tribute to Nikola Tesla, the well-known inventor, engineer, and futurist. The company was committed to developing an electric-powered car as an alternative to the more traditional fossil-fuel burning vehicles. They also wanted to be a leading name in electric technology, delivering not just a car, but battery and computer software as well. Their motivation was when General Motors discontinued all its EV1 electric motor vehicles in 2003. A few months later, Tesla Motors was founded. A short time after, Ian Wright joined Tesla as the third employee.

The very next year in February 2004, Elon joined the company when he made a substantial investment, which incidentally saw him become the chairperson of the board. He did not immediately become overly involved in the day-to-day management of the company; he did however, become very much involved in the design related activities, especially as it related to the roadster concept vehicle. The last person to join the company at this time, was Jeffrey Brian Straubel, who was appointed as the Chief Technical Officer. All five individuals would, in September 2009, eventually come to be legally recognized as equal co-founders of Tesla.

First off of the Assembly Line: The Roadster

The first vehicle that Tesla focused their attention on was the Roadster, partly due to the group all being influenced by the AC Propulsion tzero electric roadster prototype, which was an electric sports car first manufactured in the 2000s by AC Propulsion.

Elon took an active role in the design of their own Roadster, right down to the minute details such as the headlamp styling. Despite immediate conflict between Eberhard and the board, Eberhard would go on to state that Elon had been the one to insist on a carbon-fiber reinforced polymer for the body of the Roadster. Eventually in 2006, Elon received the Golden Green award for product design for the Tesla Roadster, as well as the 2007 Index Design Award.

He believed that the company's mandate was to make electric cars that would be more beneficial for the environment, but also affordable for everyone. He therefore believed that success with the Roadster would attract the correct media attention, financial backing, and popular sentiment for Tesla to next focus on more economically affordable vehicles like sedans, compacts, and even an SUV. The strategy was simple and fairly common with high-end and new technological designs: market low volumes of the product with a high purchase price to the highly affluent and niche markets. Then use the proceeds of those sales to develop and build the next model, which will then target a more moderately affluent segment of the consumer market, driving slightly higher volumes, with a slightly lower price. And then repeat the strategy until reaching the much wider mass market, with high volumes and low prices.

Then, due to the Financial Crisis of 2008, Eberhard was ousted from his position as CEO, and Elon was appointed as the new

CEO, a position which he has held to this day, which is the longest that any CEO has served in the modern automotive industry. By the end of 2008, Elon had contributed, and also raised through various investment partners, in excess of US$100 million for Tesla.

On July the 19th, 2006, a prototype of the Roadster was unveiled at a private and exclusive function. The first production lines officially began in 2008, with 2,500 units being sold to 31 different countries. The Roadster was the first electric vehicle to use a Lithium-ion battery.

Model Magic

Following the success of the Roadster's launch, Tesla then proceeded with their plan to introduce various different models, with the intention of ultimately penetrating the mass market. In January 2010, Tesla received a loan from the US Department of Energy for US$465 million, which they would go on repay by the end of 2013. After receiving the loan, Tesla went on to purchase what would eventually become its manufacturing plant, in Fremont, California in May 2010, and began designing and eventually manufacturing its second model, the Tesla Model S. That same year, Tesla listed its Initial Public Offering on the NASDAQ, becoming the first American automotive company to do so in more than half a century.

Starting with the Model S, Tesla began designing their vehicles to feature an integrated hardware and software component at the center of the vehicle, to allow for regular software updating. This then accommodates better performance and functionality for the vehicles, for free. Elon cared as much for the quality of the vehicle at the time it rolled off the showroom floor, as over the life of the vehicle. He wanted the customer experience to be the best possible. This, and other equally impressive features, has seen Tesla maintain the highest customer satisfaction rate out of the entire Automotive industry.

Two years later, in June 2012, Tesla began delivery of its Model S, for the luxury market. A few months earlier, it had launched the Model X, which catered for the SUV market; however, the delivery date was delayed by several years to 2015.

Privatization and The SEC Investigation

Another of Elon's controversial moments revolved around the investigation done by the Securities and Exchange Commission of the United States in 2018. This occurred after an announcement via Twitter that Elon was "considering taking Tesla private at $420. Funding secured." This announcement took his fans and supporters by surprise, as it was a sudden change in his entrepreneurial patterns so far and would have a huge impact on the way the company would be handled in the future.

It seemed that his declaration was taken very seriously, especially since he stated that funding was already in place. As a direct result of Elon's news, Tesla stock rose significantly, with an eventual 11% increase at the end of the day. The fallout to follow was significant, as Tesla directors spoke out that this decision had not been communicated to them and that they did not support it.

During the debate and introspection regarding whether or not Tesla would go private or continue to be a public company, the situation became even more complicated. The SEC began an investigation after Elon's original Tweet on August 7, 2018, in order to determine if he truly had secured funding for this move within the company. At this time, the SEC and those critical of Elon's business practices accused him of attempting to intentionally manipulate the stock market by making a false claim.

Throughout August, Elon made several clarifications on the source of his funding, citing potential financial relationships with Saudi Arabia, Silver Lake, and Goldman Sachs as sources of the funding he referred to. Things got more interesting when one of Elon's houseguests, popular rapper Azealia Banks, publicized that he had taken LSD and was under the influence during the time he made the original announcement on August 7. This began to overshadow the business side of the story, and social media quickly latched onto the case as a matter of celebrity intrigue.

By the end of this investigation, Elon announced that he would not in fact privatize Tesla, due to concerns from his directors and stakeholders in the company. In addition, the SEC fined him $20 million dollars and he agreed to step down as the chairman for three years.

The way this investigation was handled became a matter of further controversy for Elon's reputation and pop culture image. While he continued to innovate in his business behind the scenes, the media debated whether or not the results of the SEC investigation meant he was guilty of something malicious. Whether it was a bold business move made with the best intentions, or a misfire between financial institutions, Elon took it in stride and continued building his success even further.

New Territory

Many of Elon's ventures, companies, and investments overlap over the years. This is due to his constant need to innovate and develop new technologies for the future. Some of the best examples of this are projects that have gotten less media attention overall.

As his success climbed with Tesla, SpaceX, and everything he built before that, Elon refused to become lazy. Instead of sitting back and letting his potential go to waste, he has constantly dipped his toes into new ideas and supported innovation around him. Some of the best examples of that come from his mid 2010's investments in the SolarCity and Hyperloop projects. These are demonstrations of Elon's interest in the tech industry as a whole, and what it has to offer the future of the world.

Elon's mission statement with each of his enterprises has never been to simply make money. As someone invested in climate change, he often gets a reputation for having a negative outlook on civilization in centuries to come. Without major changes to the way people treat travel, energy, and city structure, Elon doesn't see the world staying stable forever.

Through his investments in new projects, Elon shows he plans to act on these opinions. While his work with Tesla and SpaceX already reflect an interest in sustainable tech, he also wants to focus on building better civilizations that will last longer. Elon doesn't just want to make better versions of existing technology, but new ideas that change the way cities look at transportation, energy production, and population growth.

SolarCity

One of Elon's primary focuses as a scientist and entrepreneur is sustainable energy. As a brilliant mind of this era, he has dedicated much of his work into trying to spread the use of eco-friendly products and methods. Tesla is a prime example of Elon's dedication to a green world and using his technological expertise to clean up the industry. Many of his side-projects and associated enterprises fit this same model, showing his interest in the movement.

When it comes to SolarCity, it was an easy decision for Elon to get involved. Not only did it fit into his clean energy focus, but it was a family company. His cousins, Peter and Lyndon Rive, started the company with the assistance of Elon's capital in 2006. He enabled their company to get off the ground and become one of the most prominent producers of solar energy in the United States.

SolarCity produces solar panels, roofs, installations, and more, dedicated to integrating solar energy into modern technology. In 2016, Elon further invested in SolarCity by acquiring the company and making it a subsidiary of Tesla. This enabled SolarCity to thrive financially and integrate their products with Tesla's deep roots in the tech industry. With this boost, SolarCity panels will be available for affordable rent across the U.S. in the future.

Hyperloop and The Boring Company

One of the most promising projects, introduced first in 2013, is the Hyperloop transport module. Elon envisions this as a modernized train used to revolutionize public, eco-friendly travel in the future. The Hyperloop module itself is a passenger car that travels within a vacuum sealed, subway-like tube. It maximizes the speed and efficiency of travel by reducing air resistance. According to Elon's original design, the Hyperloop could travel with 600 mph speeds from San Francisco to L.A. in a matter of 30 minutes, changing commuting as the world knows it.

Since the original announcement, Elon has done further development on the model for the Hyperloop, and began testing potential models under the SpaceX and Tesla patent in 2017. As development of the Hyperloop project began to gain traction and media attention, it became clear that this was an idea Elon was excited about.

In fact, he was so interested in seeing where this idea could take the world of transportation that he made his original design for the Hyperloop completely open source in 2013 as the idea began to gain traction. This allowed multiple companies and third-party engineers to experiment with the project and create their own potential Hyperloop pods and systems. Elon's vision often goes beyond the scope of his own personal entrepreneurship, and in this case, it allowed him to share this science with other brilliant creators around the world. This created ample competition between different Hyperloop companies, including Elon's.

SpaceX, while developing their own Hyperloop pods and tracks, fully sponsors this competitive innovation by hosting a Hyperloop Pod Competition every year. This has occurred annually from 2015-2019, judging various designs, improvements, and test-builds of Hyperloop technology in order to see what may be viable to use in reality.

Meanwhile, Elon has high hopes for Hyperloop technology to change the face of transportation across the world. He plans to use his tunneling asset, The Boring Company, to dig tracks for Hyperloop systems. As of 2018, he received permission to build tunnels in Baltimore and many locations in California. He has hopes to build systems connecting major cities in the Midwest, after thorough testing. Many tests have already shown viability for the technology to be used soon, however.

Chapter 4: The Empire that Elon Built

As a single individual and as the leader of multiple influential enterprises, Elon Musk's impact on the technological development of the modern world is enormous. The domino effect produced from Elon's early work has brought the tech industry into a new era, and he isn't finished.

This is a man with a broad scope of different interests, as evidenced by PayPal, SpaceX, Tesla, and everything in between. What they all have in common can be boiled down to Elon's drive to understand technology, enhance it, and make the world adapt to the results. In the modern era, he and his many assets have revolutionized personal transportation, clean energy, and space travel. This has laid the groundwork for a world where Elon has the means to venture into many new interests.

His success in this era has made Elon Musk a tech celebrity, to say the least. As he becomes a core engineer in the building blocks of the future, Elon proves that he can step into unfamiliar territory and offer something new.

Artificial Intelligence

One of Elon's later interests is the development of robotics. He is already well-versed in using synthetic motion and robotic machinery in the development of his smart cars, but he refused to stop at what he knew. The increased public intrigue in artificial intelligence (AI) goes hand in hand with Elon's dreams for a technological future. He has developed multiple projects in this area to begin a deep dive into the world of AI technology and innovate it.

These range from investing in modern AI-based companies, funding research into the field, to blueprinting futuristic devices with the capability of computerizing the human brain. Elon is and has always been a businessman, so many of his ventures begin with acquiring and running promising tech companies, but his influence does not stop at footing the bill. The state of modern technology would not be the same without Elon's eye for brilliance, and unending drive towards innovation.

OpenAI

In 2015, Elon Musk founded OpenAI, alongside Sam Altman and a team of other AI developers. OpenAI is a company focused on research and development of artificial intelligence, with goals to develop fully functioning AI capable of working with humans and benefiting society as a whole. The company works under multiple branches, with both a for-profit and non-profit division, to study machine learning.

Just like with Hyperloop, OpenAI has made most of its research open source. This was motivated by a desire to get insight from other organizations and institutions and make this venture collaborative with anyone who had an interest. Elon is a proponent of free information in many areas, and this contributes to his reputation as a new-age capitalist. His desire to gain information from scholars outside of his particular company drives others to create competing patents for the same technology, which in capitalist theory, makes for a higher quality product.

Elon worked with OpenAI from its founding in 2015 through 2019, when he resigned. At the time, he stated that his reason for leaving the team was due to potential conflicts between his own research into AI for Tesla's smart cars, and disagreements about the future of the company. The resignation was publicly civil, and Elon continued as a donor.

In February 2020, however, Elon was cited saying he had further issues with the security and culture of secrecy with administration at OpenAI. In particular, when questioned about the transparency and open source nature of the company since he left, he stated that he did not have faith in the safety of what was being developed. Without transparency into what OpenAI develops and how they handle the creation of more and more intelligent machines, Elon seems hesitant to increase his involvement.

Neuralink

At the turn of the decade, Neuralink is one of Elon Musk's most recent ventures into an artificially intelligent future, and it may be one of the most interesting yet. Founded in 2016, Neuralink's motivations were originally described as enhancing the human brain. This could cover goals like treating mental illness, disease, or offering transhumanist expansions to what the brain is capable of.

This would be done through the production of neuroprosthetics that could be implanted into the brain. Elon used the phrase "symbiosis with artificial intelligence" when describing long-term interests for the technology.

The Neuralink itself is a device that was demonstrated by Elon himself at an expo in August, 2020. He produced a prototype of the device, about the size of a coin, that would be fitted into the human brain in order to offer enhancements to thought processing and sensory input. While much of the development of the implant and specific intentions have been held under wraps, this display highlighted the potential direction Neuralink is headed.

The device has yet to be tested on humans but is proven to work in the minds of pigs. The way Neuralink operates is by connecting electrodes in the brain in order to boost signals, allowing information to flow more quickly.

Neuralink's potential is to make a "whole-brain interface" that allows humans to connect to the internet, cloud-based storage, and more, simply by thinking. This could allow people to truly become cyborg in nature. Elon wants to make sure that humans can enhance their own intelligence as easily as computers can, so that they aren't left behind. This falls into a field of thought called transhumanism, which focuses on improving what it means to be human in the future.

Elon's transhumanist society would revolve around Neuralink and technology like it, allowing the baseline capability of the human brain to expand beyond what any is able to perform now.

Some examples of medical uses for the Neuralink include treating stroke victims, depression, and insomnia, among other things. This would work, in theory, by using the implant to increase connections in the brain that had been lost or broken as a result of disease. Elon also demonstrated a company-wide interest in functional enhancements like playing music from the electrodes of your brain, altering your emotions, and enhancing your senses. True to himself, he has more hopes for this technology than they can possibly hold clinical trials for at this stage.

Elon's Views on AI

All of this work has not come out of nowhere. While Elon has been interested in smart technologies for years, evident by the development of Tesla's self-driving cars, this interest has not come without deep implications. Elon has demonstrated a curiosity in the technology of artificial intelligence alongside a very prominent opinion on the social ramifications of sentient computers.

While working between OpenAI and Neuralink, Elon has described his ultimate purpose to be "symbiosis" with the AI of the future. This is because he strictly believes that our future contains a prominent existence of sentient computers and independent AI. To him, this is not a sci-fi concept or even a far-off reality, but one coming up on the horizon as he studies it.

Elon has interviewed on this subject heavily, displaying a consistent view that AI is more dangerous than cute. He believes that as AI develops, virtual intelligence will soon match and eventually exceed the intelligence capable by the human brain. In a world where this becomes the norm, unchecked, Elon understands that humankind may well become endangered by the AI they created.

This opinion is highly controversial, as many researchers in the field believe this is an exaggerated and unfounded opinion of machine learning. Similarly, some AI experts call Elon's work in the field unrealistic overall, including his hopes for Neuralink technology. Just like any technological innovator, Elon is bound to have success and failure in this field, so the world may in fact be right to doubt him.

If he is to be believed, though, Elon's worst-case scenario involves the possibility of humans being pushed out of society as we know it, and potentially placed in zoo-like creations to entertain AI. He cites the way humankind took over other primates when they evolved a higher intelligence to defend this.

While this may sound like speculative fiction to most, Elon is dedicated to the concept enough to integrate it into his work. His main focus with Neuralink is to allow humankind to expand their intelligence to match the capabilities of computers. Whether or not it is truly needed to prevent a robot-run future, he believes it will benefit consumers, nonetheless.

The Cave Rescue

Elon Musk is no stranger to making news headlines, but in 2018 he took time to react to one. In response to the devastating disappearance and subsequent rescue mission of a Thai soccer team, Elon worked with Tesla engineers to develop a specialized submarine intended to go into the cave. He brought the submarine across the world and delivered it in person to the rescue mission, bringing a great amount of attention with him.

The events that followed were chaotic and controversial, putting Elon at the center of a disaster that originally had nothing to do with him. From the original disappearance to the final rescue of the team, Elon's involvement gained public praise and criticism. Well after the situation was resolved, he continued engaging with the Thai rescue team due to ongoing media attention.

Background

From June through July 2018, a group of twelve teenaged soccer players and their 25-year old assistant coach were known across the world as they were stranded, trapped inside a flooded cave system in Chang Rai, Thailand. While the details are widely disputed by witnesses, the media widely reported that the soccer team had gone into the caves together after practice, led by their assistant coach.

Soon after entering the caves, heavy flooding blocked them into the caves, and they could not escape. Their rescue was initially delayed due to the fact that their location was unknown and unreported before the disappearance. Parents of the children did not know they would be visiting the cave system, and the flooding prevented them from calling for help. They were ultimately located by making contact with one of the boys via cellphone and locating their abandoned bags outside of the cave system.

Over the course of 18 days, a search and rescue mission was created and enacted. A cave expert by the name of Vern Unsworth led the operation due to knowledge of the caves among other certifications. A team of divers spent nine days searching the caves with no luck before the children were finally located, but it was not solved that easily. From there, multiple operations were presented to get them out.

Due to the nature of the cave and the flooding, there were limited options to retrieve the team safely. Experts considered teaching them to dive and provide equipment, while also debating whether or not waiting until the end of flooding season would be easier.

Ultimately, the boys were rescued on July 8th through an intricate operation where several divers entered the caves and guided each boy out individually with professional equipment. All thirteen trapped individuals were rescued, though there was one fatality among the divers.

The Submarine

Throughout this process, the disaster had gained international attention due to the severity of the issue. During this time, Elon became aware of the issue, and many of his supporters inquired if he could create a solution to the problem. This became a new focus for Elon, and after publicly theorizing a few ways they could retrieve the boys from the cave, he settled on manufacturing a kid-sized submarine.

This was a small 5-foot long, 12-foot wide submarine meant to hold one child at a time and be piloted manually by two adult divers. The submarine was named "Wild Boar" to match the soccer team and mascot by the same name. After assembling a team of engineers from The Boring Company and SpaceX, he had a submarine designed and built within 8 hours. At this time, a rescue operation was already beginning, but divers on the team requested the submarine be sent as a back-up method regardless.

The submarine was engineered by experts at Elon's disposal, using an oxygen tube from a Falcon 9 space vehicle.

By the time the device was delivered, eight of the twelve boys had already been reportedly rescued. It was not used during the rescue, but Elon was recognized in 2019 by the King of Thailand for his efforts regardless.

The Unsworth Trial and Fallout

While that was the end of the terrible event for the victims involved and most of the public, Elon continued to be involved for much longer after that. In the time following the event, many media outlets had praised Elon Musk, SpaceX, and The Boring Company for their efforts and invention created to rescue the soccer team. This garnered quite a big spotlight on Elon after the rescue had been completed without the submarine, and as a result, many of the divers on the team were questioned about it.

This is where Vern Unsworth became critically involved with Elon's story. Unsworth was a lead diver for most of the rescue mission as an expert British caver. When interviewed publicly, he stated that the submarine was not used, not only because of when it was delivered, but because it was useless to the mission.

He described it as a public relations stunt overall, with more intent to make Elon Musk look good than to rescue the children. Unsworth went on to insist that the submarine was made by someone who had no understanding of what the cave was like, and said Elon could "stick his submarine where it hurts."

The backlash that followed caused additional controversy that Elon would not be able to escape quickly. Over Twitter, he published a series of comments on the statement, referring to Unsworth as a "pedo guy", and implying that he looked like or may be a criminal pedophile. These comments were deleted later, and Elon ultimately admitted he had released them in anger, with no intent of slandering Unsworth.

This did not end things so easily, though. Unsworth and Elon responded publicly over the issue back and forth, with escalating accusations. Unsworth was allegedly harassed, defamed, and investigated for crimes he did not commit under no basis of evidence, while Elon continued to double-down on his comments publicly in order to defend his stance.

At one point in August 2018, Elon engaged with the subject further on Twitter by stating that it was suspicious that Unsworth had not sued him for defamation. He indicated that this was a sign he was likely guilty, and that a lawsuit would bring attention to it. In September 2018, Unsworth did sue, citing 65 pages with exhibits of defamation, but Elon was found not liable.

When the verdict came through in his favor, Elon stated his faith in humanity had been restored.

American Politics

To finish off a decade of diversification to Elon's career, in 2016 he elevated from tech celebrity to tech representative. Throughout the 2016 presidential election, Elon was hesitant to declare his political position. For some time, he was skeptical of Donald Trump's potential to be a successful president, but by the time he was inaugurated, he came out in support of his financial policies.

Elon Musk describes himself as "half Democrat, half Republican," due to his mixed political opinions. Because of this, he has not shown consistent partisanship when his business ventures cross paths with those of the U.S. Government.

In 2016, he accepted a position on Donald Trump's business advisory council as a forum-member. He, along with 17 other members, were appointed to guide presidential decisions on economics and other issues for the country's well-being. Being a controversial election, Elon defended his position by stating he wanted the president to be well-advised throughout his term, from a number of different voices. This included his own.

By 2017, however, Elon resigned from the council after Trump's decision to leave the Paris Agreement. Elon highly disagreed with the President's move away from a focus on climate change, which to him, was the most important issue.

Chapter 5: The Future is Elon Musk

There is no clear end in sight when it comes to Elon Musk's ever-growing path to success. Whether or not he continues to rise in fame, fortune, and fascination is up to him. That being said, it seems as if he has a never-ending pool of ideas for what to do next.

As of 2020, Elon has refused to slow down. For each of his current projects, he has plans for how they'll look in the future. When it comes to newer investments like Neuralink and Hyperloop, the future is now. These enterprises have just gotten off the ground when it comes to modern machinery, and they have a lot of room to grow.

That's not to say that Elon isn't investing in his core companies. In fact, SpaceX and Tesla have multiple projects in the works that come with a lot of implications about what the world looks like with Elon Musk at the wheel.

Cities of the Future

Space colonization is a hot topic when it comes to Elon himself, his supporters, and associates. SpaceX has made a number of interesting moves towards Mars exploration, including rocket innovations and launch technology. Beyond that, Elon has made it clear that his final goal is to assist colonization of Mars and create a variety of technologies to make the planet inhabitable.

In addition, Elon has covered the idea of underground tunnels as the way of the future, even beyond the scope of flying cars. He's discussed the merits of digging underground systems to promote high speed travel and even more technological extensions, and how they differ from space/air travel. When it comes to the future, Elon has investments in both the sky and the soil.

SpaceX and Mars

One of Elon Musk's oldest fascinations is with building space cities, most realistically on Mars. In recent history, he has been discussing this issue with more realistic ventures in mind. With prospective missions to Mars in the near future, having an upper hand on the technology involved in colonization is right within Elon's wheelhouse.

Speaking in 2019, Elon musk stated that by 2050 he wants to see millions of people landing on Mars. This follows his goals to get a cargo rocket to Mars by 2022, and a follow-up ship by 2024. While these dates are relatively speculative, they indicate an ongoing plan from SpaceX to develop the necessary technologies needed to begin the first stages of colonization, or at least investigation, on Mars.

Elon has prioritized Mars as one of his long-term goals. Some of the prospects for his idealized Mars city include a direct democracy, surplus of jobs, and enclosed structures. These interests drive him towards developing more powerful longevity systems in his spaceships and the sustainable resources to get them to Mars in large quantities, with consistent reinforcement supplies over time.

This is why logistics is one of Elon's prime focuses when it comes to Mars living. In an interview with CNBC on his plans for colonization, Elon elaborated on the amount of micromanaging he must do in order to structure these plans.

"In order to make something self-sustaining, you can't be missing anything. You must have all the ingredients. It can't be like, well this thing is self-sustaining except for this one little thing that we don't have. It can't be. That'd be like saying, 'Well … we had everything except vitamin C.' OK, great. Now you're going to get scurvy and die—and painfully, by the way. It's going to suck. You're going to die slowly and painfully for lack of vitamin C. So, we've got to make sure we've got the vitamin C there on Mars."

Underground Tunnels

When some doubt the possibility of colonizing other planets in the near future, Elon has more to offer. The ideas of flying cars and jet-stream food trucks may seem appealing to others, but Elon has pointed out that many real citizens may find them disruptive. From noise pollution to road clog, vehicles have their limits. Elon envisions a future where underground roadways dominate long-term transport, including both air vacuum tunnel pods akin to the Hyperloop and even more niche prospects like subsoil highways that advanced Tesla models can handle.

Elon has stated that he spends around 3-4% of his time managing The Boring Company, but it sets roots for a lot of his investments in the future. The idea of building Hyperloop systems to travel between distant regions, or give new eco-friendly locations for cars to commute, all require underground tunneling. These tunnels, of course, are only possible with the technological innovations brought into being by The Boring Company and likeminded engineers.

When critics have asked about long-term solutions to underground transport tunnels, specifically to the limits of Hyperloop and other train tubes, Elon has the solutions. When it comes to the possibility of congestion, he proposes additional layers of tunnels, going deeper underground. This shows the infinite possibility of underground development in the modern era, especially in opposition to air travel.

Tesla Innovations

Most of the public can agree that more cars are in Elon's future. After everything Tesla has introduced to the future of vehicle innovation, he isn't stopping any time soon. Tesla's reign over automobile tech comes from their consistent ability to stay at the forefront of the newest ideas. They did it with electric motors, sleek seamless design, and self-driving cars. As of 2020, Elon already has his prospects set for the horizon for what he wants out of new Tesla models.

New items down the line include the Model Y crossover and the new Roadster sports car. These are both luxury Tesla vehicles with a futuristic design and updates to autopilot systems. In November of 2019, the Cybertruck took the world by storm as the hottest new toy coming out of Tesla Motors. The sci-fi looking truck is a different feel for Tesla, meant for towing heavy loads with energy efficiency. More trucks may be coming down the line, with promises of a clean energy Tesla semi in the future.

These, alongside other new models, will go into production at one of Tesla's many plants being built in 2020 and 2021 across the U.S. With greater manufacturing capacity, many Americans hope Teslas will become more approachable, affordable, and replace their clunky counterparts completely in the next few decades.

Philanthropy

As Elon's empire has grown, he has become a staple to the U.S. economy, tech industry, and pop culture. In a time when the billionaires of the world have garnered a lot of attention for hoarding wealth and polluting the environment, Elon continues to reinvest his money into the earth itself. While the environment deteriorates and gets closer to devastating long-term effects for civilization, Elon's focus on climate change has led him to look again to the future of humankind.

Alongside other humanitarian efforts, Elon provided aid in 2018 to the Flint, Michigan water crisis. He used a donation of $480,000 to build and provide water filtration systems and install them across the city, offering much needed relief from the polluted drinking water. By 2019, a measured 30,000 children had access to clean water as a result of these installations.

Elon has also made significant donations to the #TeamTrees initiative, totaling in $1 million as of 2019. TeamTrees is a group sponsored by the Arbor Day Foundation, focused on planting millions of trees to naturally clean up our atmosphere and promote forest life.

COVID-19 Crisis

Throughout the Coronavirus pandemic, beginning in 2020, Elon has been an active voice on the subject. His opinions on the virus itself were highly controversial, indicating that he did not believe it was a threat to him or many Americans, and that an economical lockdown was a bad idea. He was prominently against the mandated business closures that shut down his Tesla manufacturing centers due to the impact it had on his business.

Like many Americans early on, Elon first believed the virus was not dangerous to young people or otherwise healthy individuals. This impacted his decisions to attempt to keep some of his businesses operating after the lockdown mandates, resulting in negative responses from the public.

Despite this, Elon also focused on offering aid and engineering solutions to help curb the virus. As more information became known about COVID-19 itself, Elon's opinions became less focused on undermining the virus, and more on solving it. In April 2020, Tesla provided significant donations of CPAP machines to developing countries in need. He also indicated that Tesla would be producing their own model of ventilator to help make medical treatment of the virus more available and successful in the future.

The Future is Now

It's hard to imagine the dawn of the new millennium without Elon Musk as a key figure. With the vast enterprises he has already created, his mind has already been integrated into modern society in ways that will impact innovation to come. He has intentionally spread his reach across multiple industries, including economic policy, space travel, infrastructure, and medicine.

SpaceX marks the beginning of practical space travel, and has already laid the groundwork for what is possible outside the reaches of planet earth. When humans land on Mars for the first time, Elon believes it will be in a SpaceX rover, or at the very least, one inspired by its design. He plans to make it possible for humans to arrive on Mars in droves, and also to build the infrastructure to keep them alive between shipments. Eventually, this could make it possible for humankind to spread wide beyond Mars and even the Milky Way.

The work Elon has done with Hyperloop, The Boring Company, and Tesla shows he hasn't left earth behind. While he has his eyes on the sky, he has his mind on the ground, investing deeper into underground tunnels as long-term solutions for city life. Elon sees a future where high-speed trains can zip someone across the country in a matter of hours, and crowded cities can continue to grow down beneath the surface. In a world threatened by climate change and environmental destruction, Elon is prepared to save it by thinking outside, under, and above the box.

Most people have a difficult time seeing too far beyond their own lifespan. Knowing what things will be like for children and grandchildren down the line is impossible, so planning for it is hard. Elon has taken that job upon himself, dedicating his mind, wealth, and work ethic to building the world of the future.

Conclusion

Ultimately, Elon Musk's tumultuous history through technological innovation and celebrity impact will leave a mark on humankind forever. This man has proven that his mind is one of a kind, and that it processes the world differently than the average genius.

From humble, if not dreadful beginnings, Elon's story epitomizes the American dream. Despite the turmoil of his upbringing, from his complicated relationship with his father to the community that rejected him, Elon chose to build up a tough skin and focus on bettering himself for it all.

While he plans for the future of the world itself, his own life is changing every day. It can be easy to forget that the man behind the machines is just that: a man. As the world poses more problems for him to solve, his own family remains reliant on him as a partner and father, not an engineer. Elon's many children, including the newborn X Æ A-Xii, will grow up in a world their father helped shape.

There is no clear sign if Elon will ever settle down and find his way out of the limelight. He still has a lot of dreams, and plenty of resources to make them happen. How his story ends will directly impact how he is remembered for years to come, but he will be remembered, nonetheless. Elon Musk is one of the most extraordinary, controversial, and influential individuals the world has ever known, and in his mind, he is only just getting started.